# The labyrinth
# INFLUENCE

*"If you want to find the secrets
of the universe, think in terms of energy,
frequency and vibrations."*
—Nikola Tesla

# The labyrinth INFLUENCE

## AWAKEN THE WISDOM WITHIN

Based on a true story of self-transformation

# PJ JACKSON

For speaking inquiries, to purchase the book in bulk, or to schedule time to talk with the author, PJ Jackson, please contact Connect@PJJackson.com.

For more information, visit www.PJJackson.com

Library of Congress Control Number:  2018944937

ISBN Paperback: 978-1-947341-19-7
ISBN eBook: 978-1-947341-20-3

Printed in the United States of America

Book Design: Redwood Publishing, LLC

*To all the women who ask,*
*"Am I doing this right?"*

# Preface

*O*nce upon a time there was a Woman, tormented by her success. The harder she worked, the more work she was given. Whenever someone else could not get the job done, she stepped in and saved the day. Her career grew strong, her reputation traveled far, and yet, even with all her credentials and accolades, the Woman felt unfulfilled.

Success can be a monster, addictive and cold when you have lost your purpose—when you are blindly following someone else's agenda. For the Woman, thirty years of success had now rewarded her with a stroke and a pink slip.

Then one day a friend gave her a note. It read:

*All the success in the world cannot satisfy divine discontent. You are looking for something more.*

This idea of divine discontent was foreign to her. Not knowing how it could help her, the Woman did the only thing she knew how to do: She continued to excel and succeed, until one day a third catastrophe struck, and she was forced to slow down. Her husband was now deathly ill.

# Introduction

*W*hen you were young, did you ever dream about your path in life? Did you wonder what you would be when you grew up, consider the things that you would make, the places you would go, and the people you would meet?

Maybe, as you patched up stuffed animal after stuffed animal in the makeshift hospital of your living room, you imagined being a world-class doctor, treating children around the globe. Or you longed to be an in-demand fashion designer, sketching outfits for Barbie's every sartorial need.

Perhaps you thought about what your childhood best friend would look like as an adult—still your partner. in crime after so many years. Together, you'd be running the business you'd fantasized about in each other's backyards and bedrooms.

Maybe you pictured the view from atop a ski slope in the Alps, the Eiffel Tower, or even a camel—the dust of the desert spreading out before you as far as your eyes could see.

Youth is filled with dreams that make our hearts soar. Grand visions fill you with a joyful sense of wonder about what lies ahead when you are grown.

You make a plan and set your course, visualizing the steps needed to reach your goal. Finally, you feel confident enough to share it with others. You want their insights; you want to know if your ideas are as inspiring to them as they are to you. All you seek is some validation that you've chosen an acceptable path, and that those closest to you believe in the value of your aspirations.

Unfortunately, your plans and dreams don't always align with those of the people who love you. They suggest other goals, pointing out all the ways you could fall short if you attempt to achieve something so risky—or frivolous—as your own vision. They tell you, "It would be so great if you just did X or Y or Z."

You begin to see the flaws in your plan. How silly it was of you to think you'd chosen the right path! So instead of dreaming big or setting your sights on something they've deemed insignificant, you pick what you feel you are supposed to do: a college that will make your family proud, a job that will come with financial success, a series of logical steps that don't draw too much attention or make too much noise.

Ever since you were a little girl, the world taught you how to play by the rules: Work harder than anyone else and you will be rewarded. Don't accentuate that fact you are a woman; act like a man to be successful in business. But don't take up too much space. When setting your priorities, always put yourself last. This is what makes a successful woman.

Sitting at your desk years later, looking at your perfectly prioritized to-do list, you have this overwhelming sense that no matter how many hours you put in this week, no matter how much planning you do, something will still blow up, and you will have to pick up the pieces.

You wake up in the morning, unrested and anxious from those spinning to-dos the night before. You have to focus on getting ready for work, yet you can't seem to get out the door. Your stomach is tied up in knots and nothing seems to relieve the stress. You drag yourself to the shower, get dressed, and finally make it out with minutes to spare before you're officially late. Looming before you is another day of the status quo: the same slow-creeping, bumper-to-bumper drive, and a schedule so packed that you wouldn't have had the time to eat that yogurt you accidentally left on the counter, even if you'd remembered it.

After a full day of traffic jams, rushing to meaningless meetings, and navigating office drama so petty and coworkers so judgmental that your head is about to explode, you make it home with barely enough time to put a meal on the table.

Now it's late in the evening. The dishes are washed, the kids are in bed, and the bills are paid. Miraculously, you find that you have some free time. What do you do?

You immediately turn to that to-do list to accomplish something for someone else.

You'll spend the few precious hours left in the day putting the finishing touches on your daughter's Halloween costume, fulfilling your boss's urgent request, or organizing some cluttered corner of your home.

Does this sound like you?

Some people would call you a superwoman. In fact, you may feel rather proud that you can juggle it all. You can work full time, go to school to get that next degree, keep your kids on the honor roll, please your spouse, and be an active member of the community. You may even be grateful that others have noticed. Why? Because you were conditioned that way. You've been told by the world that you yourself are less important than the "contributions" you make to the world.

This was the path that those who loved you when you were young said was right, logical, fulfilling. They chose it for you, and you accepted. This is what you were expected to do with your life, and you're doing it masterfully!

But what if—just what *if*—you could change that conditioning and still be happy and successful? What would you want to change?

Would you put in fewer hours at the office, or build a different career altogether? Would you deepen your relationship with your spouse? Or would you spend more time by yourself, pursuing the passions you had as a girl, the ones you once thought would drive your life's work?

You already have the knowledge you need to get to the core of the person you've always wanted to be—the person you've been all along. All you need to do is access it. You can learn the art of awakening the wisdom within. It's part of who you are, who you have always been. You can live a life of balance, a life in which every day is truly *lived* with grace, power, and ease. You *can* awaken the wisdom within!

But first, you have to learn how to nurture yourself, to find out what you already know, and trust that whatever it is, it is right for you.

Taking time for yourself may be something you've never really done before, a consideration that always seemed frivolous at best and selfish at worst—a need you imagine you assuage with an occasional haircut or a good book or a short walk. Self care—and self awareness—need to be a way of life. This isn't selfish; it's essential. We can start here.

If you are looking to figure out how to regain control of your life and how to be blissfully happy in every aspect of it, then welcome to your new path. You have come to the right place.

*Chapter One*

Seen from the outside looking in, the Woman's life was charmed. Having spent time in the navy seeing the world, she had accumulated her fair share of memorable experiences. She had always striven for academic excellence, and in the process, she'd acquired sufficient knowledge and expertise to become one of the leaders in her field, and to be nationally recognized for her contributions to it. If that weren't enough, the

Woman continued to go to school at night while working full time to earn yet another title: *applied scientist*.

Sought after to speak about and facilitate change at the highest corporate levels, she never stopped to look back. Whenever someone else could not get the job done, she stepped in and saved the day. Her schedule was filled with travel and speaking engagements, ranging from intimate meetings with a handful of space engineers to auditoriums crowded with an entire company's employees—hundreds of people leaning forward to listen to her latest stories from the field. The Woman was on fire!

Her personal life seemed enviable, too: She had a sprawling house surrounded by serene woods and scenic mountains, a kind, handsome husband, and a daughter primed to go on to the Naval Academy. She was living the dream, in all its white-picket-fence glory, further bolstered by her remarkable professional achievements.

But success came at a cost. That beautiful home life was always on the back burner. Her once rotational travel schedule—one week on the road, one off—gradually became more intense, and soon she found herself spending just a few days each week with her husband and family before she was off saving the world once more. When she arrived home, her arms laden with presents from the airport and hotel gift shops of her far-flung travels, her daughter would greet her wearily, asking when she'd be leaving again. She was weary too: at the peak of her success, her pace measured sixty speaking engagements in less than one year.

Sure, she was tired, but how could she stop? The requests for her expertise continued to arrive every day. People knew her name; they wanted her to help them change the world.

She felt she was making a difference. Isn't that what we are all taught to do—find a career that you can excel at, and be a high performer, no matter the stakes?

* * *

It was Election Day, and the Woman had just enough time to cast her vote before jumping on a plane. She was scheduled to lead a complex interactive event—her specialty. She knew she was the right person for the job, and she was proud to have landed the opportunity. The first day had been as exhilarating as it was exhausting—she'd gone directly to the event from the airport—and she was grateful to retire to her hotel room that night and watch the election results pour in. She was asleep before half the states were tallied.

She awoke the next morning, before her alarm as usual. But when she tried to get up, the Woman noticed something strange: Her right side was paralyzed and numb. She rolled onto her side to reach her phone, and dialed her husband.

"Hi, honey," she said calmly when he picked up. "I'm not feeling right. My side is totally numb. Maybe it's because of the way I slept? It'll be a little difficult to drive to work; what do you think I should do?"

"I think you should go to the emergency room," he said, surprised at her lack of concern. "Now."

Instead, the Woman decided to take a shower. Maybe this would go away by the time she was finished and she could make it to work on time. Standing under the water, her weight resting on the foot she could feel, gripping the soap with her left hand, the Woman continued to believe this would fix itself. She believed the numbness would just go away, because she needed to go to work today—people were counting on her.

Unfortunately, her condition did not change. Begrudgingly, the Woman put on her yoga clothes, grabbed her purse, and headed to the lobby to request a taxi. "Where would you like to go?" the concierge asked, to which the Woman responded, "The closest emergency room."

What transpired next was not what the Woman was expecting. She was hoping she'd be dismissed upon her arrival after being diagnosed with a migraine, or even dehydration—something easily fixed. But the nurses ran some tests and told her she would need to rest until the results came back. She lay on her gurney, frustrated. At this rate, she wouldn't even make it to the after-breakfast breakout sessions.

The Woman contacted her coworkers, apologizing for her absence, and assured them she was feeling better. "I am sure I will be back later today," she told her team. On the television in front of her, the morning news turned to daytime talk shows, then the late-afternoon soap operas. The results were never delivered.

The Woman asked to speak to someone in charge. By this time the emergency room staff was changing shifts, and the evening crew was coming on board. The five o'clock news detailed an approaching storm, a string of local robberies, the newfound dangers of a common household product, and of course, the previous day's election. A doctor the Woman had never seen before showed up at her hospital bed. "When will I be able to leave?" the Woman asked.

"You aren't going anywhere," the doctor responded. "You've had a stroke."

The doctor began to describe the consequences of a stroke—the interruption of blood flow to a part of the brain, causing the death of brain cells in that area. It would take time, he said, to determine how severe her stroke had been.

The woman's mind flashed to her teammates, who were leading the workshop she had designed. She imagined the event's proceedings, which were going on without her even now, her coworkers mingling with their clients at dinner, as the doctor reviewed her case. She thought about all she'd miss in the coming weeks as she recovered. She pictured herself laid up in bed, her family trying to care for her in addition to their other responsibilities.

The doctor informed her that her husband was on a plane at that moment, on his way to her bedside. "Don't you worry," he said.

But she *was* worried. How could she not be? Up until this point in her life, she had been successful because she could use her mind in a way few others could. If she was not able to think and act like herself, what could she do? Work defined the Woman, and without it, she felt she was of no value. How would she move forward? What would her life be like?

She wasn't ready to give up. While on her six weeks of medical leave, the Woman spent hours each day doing computer-based mental tasks to strengthen her brain, thinking that if she could improve her score, she could return to work. Slowly, she rebuilt the functionality she had lost. She was relieved—her purpose could remain intact! But upon her return to work, the Woman would only be challenged once more.

A new year had arrived, and with it, new performance objectives. The Woman felt great! She had successfully rejoined her team, who welcomed her with open arms—and put her right back on the road. Soon she was contributing even more than she had before, and traveling just as much. The Woman was grateful to be doing what she believed was her calling. She was on her path, making a difference.

Seven days into the new year, she received an urgent e-mail from her boss. "Everyone on the phone in fifteen minutes," it said, all in the subject line. *How exciting,* the Woman thought, *there must be some big project!* The Woman and her team filed into the office conference room. She took a seat at the center of the table, waiting for instructions, ready to give it her all. The phone at the center of the table began to ring, and she pressed the speaker button.

Her boss's voice flooded the room. "Okay," he said. "No need to draw this out. The department's being liquidated. You each have thirty days to find a new role in the company or you're gone."

*What? I am one of the best at what I do,* the Woman thought. *This can't be happening to me*. After years of working hard, giving 110 percent, delivering more than most, and being on the road more than she had been home, the Woman was now looking for a new job. On top of that, she would have to compete against the fifty other high performers who were also being laid off. The line went dead, replaced by the anxious murmurings of her coworkers echoing off the conference room walls. She walked out in a daze.

Once again, the Woman's identity was called into question. Up until this point in her life she never really had to interview for a job; she'd joined the navy at an early age and been picked up by a navy contractor shortly after her discharge. She'd excelled in every job she'd ever had, and her expertise was continually sought out by new leaders with new roles for her. Now the Woman needed to reconsider her life yet again and figure out how to move forward.

There is only so much turmoil a person can handle, and the Woman had been given her fair share. Not knowing how else to deal with her situation, she did the only thing she knew how to do: She continued to work. While everyone else was interviewing for new jobs, the Woman continued to support her client. While the rest of her team members abandoned their regular work, shirking their responsibilities to submit applications and prepare presentations on their many specialized skills, the Woman continued to deliver on her promises. She knew that something would turn up if only she kept working hard.

She was right. Just before her termination date, the Woman received two job offers on the same day. Finally, something positive was happening.

The Woman took the more attractive of the two offers and maintained her dedication to her work, acutely cognizant of the importance of pleasing her new employer. But as time passed, something began to stir inside her. Her desire to climb the corporate ladder began to wane. The energy she had always thrived on seemed to thrum incessantly, like the buzz of a faulty fluorescent bulb. She pushed the grating feeling away on planes, in meetings, and at conferences and presentations, as she confidently strode across stages around the world. Still, the low, uncomfortable hum began to permeate her dreams.

One weekend an old friend came to visit. They had served in the navy together, and her friend had her own prestigious career. But after years of travel along her high-powered route, her friend had traded in her business suits for a new wardrobe of drapey flax and soft linen: She had become a yoga teacher and massage therapist. She practiced out of a little studio that she'd built onto the back of her house, where she spent the vast majority of her time. "I haven't been on a plane in a year!" she giggled.

They had a wonderful time, reminiscing about all they had done together. The Woman couldn't help but notice a lightness in her friend that hadn't been there before. On the last night of their visit, the Woman briefly confided in her friend about the buzzing feeling before quickly brushing it off. "I still love what I do," she finished, "I'm lucky to be doing it, especially after all I've been through."

Her friend nodded, gently touching her shoulder. "I get it," she said.

The next day, after her friend left, the Woman went up to her guest room to straighten up. She found the bed stripped and remade, the sheets folded in a neat pile on top of the duvet. On one of the pillows, her friend had left a note:

*All the success in the world cannot satisfy divine discontent. You are looking for something more.*

The Woman slid the note into the pocket of her jeans. Once in a while, she imagined it hanging in her closet, quietly calling to her.

* * *

It was late in the evening a few months later. The day had been jam-packed: She was busy putting together a new project, and she had slipped into her usual flow, the hours flying by like minutes. The light outside had gotten thin, the shadows of the streetlamps stretching long across the parking lot, where only a few cars still lingered. She noticed she was squinting in the sudden dimness and stopped what she was doing to look around her office.

Her desk lamp highlighted the bright white of the ever-growing stack of papers in front of her awaiting her review and approval. Her in-box seemed to ping every minute with a new request. Her walls were adorned with awards acknowledging her many contributions to her field. An assistant sat just outside her door, ready and willing to help her take on the world.

She even had a mini espresso bar in her office, outfitted with a tiny refrigerator to keep her milk chilled, a frother, vanilla syrup, and French café cups, so she didn't have to leave the executive floor to get her cappucino fix. The arrangement had originally been a bit of a thrill—to think of herself as so important that the world could stop for *her* every once in a while, instead of the other way around, even for something as trivial as a cappucino.

But today, in her darkening office, her work brain clouding with thoughts of the meal she'd defrost when she finally got home, and whether she could make it to the last act her daughter's play if she took the highway instead of the local route, she couldn't make sense out of why she was doing what she was doing. What was the point of all this?

Deep down inside, she knew she needed to change; the spotlight above her had been on for so long, and the Woman was hot. The term *burned out* resonated more every day. Lately, she couldn't stop thinking about the note her friend had left behind: *You are looking for something more.* Maybe she was. Maybe she needed to go somewhere else to find it. So the Woman began to contemplate leaving.

She broached the subject with her husband one night. They relished the nights they got to spend in the same bed—he lying on his side, facing her, his arm draped around her underneath the warmth of their down comforter. "Honey, can we talk about something?" she asked. He nodded at her encouragingly, so she continued. "Work has been so much lately.

I feel like it's all I do. I miss you. I miss our daughter. What would you think about me leaving, or maybe just taking a break—taking some time to figure out my next step?"

He rolled onto his back and stared at the ceiling fan, quiet for a moment. "I'm not sure how we could make that work, sweetheart," he said. "You make a lot of money—much more than I do—and we have so much debt. Plus, this job is relatively new; you told me just the other day how much you liked it. I think you need to stay and make the best of it for now. I'm sorry." And with that, he kissed her cheek and turned out the light.

This was not the reaction she had hoped for.

When she mentioned her possible exit to a senior mentor over lunch, the mentor told the Woman to keep it to herself. "No one needs to know you are thinking about leaving," the mentor told her, forking another bite of salad. "They will lose faith in you."

The Woman finally gave in to the voices of those around her. They were probably right, anyway. She had worked so hard, had been given so much. And she had only just recovered from not one, but two setbacks, hadn't she?

Only a short time ago she had been so grateful to be back on track. Grateful even to be able to work again after the terrifying experience of the stroke. To have a job at all after a round of sudden layoffs. How could she even contemplate throwing it all away over some vague sense of unfulfillment? People were counting on her. She had bills to pay, a family to take care of. What was she thinking? Maybe this was some kind of midlife crisis.

The Woman decided to stay the course. She continued to be successful in her new job, checking off boxes left and right, her responsibilities stacking up like plates waiting to be washed. But one day she would no longer have a choice. Her choice was going to be made for her. She had weathered the stroke and the loss of her job, but unbeknownst to her, a third challenge was waiting for her in the wings.

# Chapter Two

Mother Nature is extremely kind to provide the opportunity for such delight and wonder in the changing of the seasons. The passing of time and the shifts in our surroundings can create an incredible swell of emotions, triggered differently for each of us.

For some, winter means the comfort of a warm fire crackling in a fireplace, thousands of twinkling lights all aglow, and hot cocoa soothing the soul; others only notice the cold.

Spring brings rebirth throughout the natural world: tight green buds on once-bare trees, the eager peeping of hatchlings in their nests. And yet, some only experience the rain drenching their hopes and dreams. Summer can bring with it memories of childhood's most carefree moments—though some remain fixated on the oppressive heat.

And then there is autumn, with its crisp air and the smell of freshly fallen leaves. It's hard not to feel like something wonderful is right around the corner, even if only the bitterness of winter awaits.

Autumn had come and gone twice since the Woman's stroke, and she was ready for a break—something lovely to distract her busy mind and lull her into a sense of calm, no matter how temporary. Stealing away on a Saturday morning, the Woman and her husband took their convertible roadster out for a ride through the mountains to have brunch at their favorite café. She loved this drive—the soft ripple of the landscape, the halos of sunlight that shone through the clouds, and the endless breadth of the sky.

It was still early, and the parking lot was almost empty when they pulled into their usual spot and clambered out of the car. The Woman smiled at the familiar tinkle of chimes as the café door closed behind them.

They were greeted with open arms by their favorite waitress, who had become a family friend and had not seen the couple in months.

It's funny how life flies by when you are living it. We go through cycles of awareness; whatever we focus on gets the bulk of our energy. Caught up in how happy the waitress was to see them, the Woman could immerse herself in the interaction with a level of awareness she had tucked away for many months. Instead of pulling her phone from her purse and checking for messages, she was in the moment, noticing every detail: the radiating warmth of the little restaurant, the smell of freshly brewed coffee and buttery baked goods, the hug the waitress was giving her husband.

Watching them embrace, however, the Woman noticed a frailness in her husband's stance, even a lack of balance. He seemed to have to work to keep himself upright. His skin looked pale, thin almost.

After they slid into their booth, the Woman asked him, "When is the last time you had your numbers checked?" The Woman's husband was a leukemic in remission, and had been for thirteen years. But today, something was different—off. She was concerned. If she had not been paying attention—if she had stopped to check her phone or even busied herself with the menu—the moment that captured her attention might have come and gone without her even noticing.

"I don't know, why?" her husband responded.

"You don't look well," she whispered. "You should make an appointment to see if everything is okay."

The Woman's husband did as he was asked and went to see his doctor, who ran some tests. After two tense weeks, the results arrived. The doctor's response was troubling: "Maybe you should follow up with your oncologist."

Panic set in. The Woman thought back over all those years since he had last been ill, desperately trying to remember what the numbers meant, and what, if anything, she could glean from the figures in front of her.

"Instead of playing doctor, why don't we call someone?" her husband asked.

Three days later, the Woman's husband had a bone marrow biopsy, the results of which confirmed her intuition: Her husband's leukemia had returned. Instead of packing for her next business trip, the Woman was now packing them up to move into the hospital.

* * *

How do you decide what to bring when you're going away? If your job requires frequent travel, you might have a checklist of the standard stuff you need to make life on the road more relaxing—like warm socks for the always-chilly plane ride, or shower products with a scent that reminds you of home. If you're headed out on vacation, you might buy a few new outfits suitable for the climate and culture of an exotic destination.

But when you are moving back into a hospital to fight for your husband's life, what do you take with you?

Family memories, familiar comforts, and faith. Pictures of those you love and mementos that bring joy. Blankets and music to create a cozy and uplifting environment among blankness and sterility. Optimism—you have been down this road before and survived, and you'll make it through again. The belief that everything happens for a reason, even when you have no idea what this journey will bring and why you're being tested once again.

Christmas came with a video fireplace. New Year's brought a flutter of rainbow confetti against starched white sheets. Now spring was here, the crocuses poking up through ice-encrusted soil outside the husband's hospital window.

"If we find out that I am going to die this time," the husband said to the Woman one day, "maybe you should stop working." The Woman had dreamed of leaving her industry, but never like this.

Still, she didn't hesitate to respond, "How about you live, and I retire?"

Not knowing where life would take them over the next week, let alone the coming months, the Woman finally let go of the career she had built and became her husband's full-time caregiver. But letting go wasn't as easy as she thought it would be.

She had to train others to take over her job—in fact, she had to try to teach them to *be* her. She had to give away all her trade secrets to help her teammates succeed, and it hurt—more than she expected. With each insight she provided, she felt as if she were disappearing a little bit, the most valuable parts of her being replaced.

When she left work early each day to head back to the hospital, she imagined the office chugging along without her, her teammates employing the strategies she'd carefully honed over the years. She pictured her replacement standing in her office, determining how to arrange their belongings on her desk.

On the last day that her office still belonged to her, she finished taking down the diplomas and awards that hung on her walls. Bright white squares were left behind, hinting at all that she'd be taking with her, and potentially packing away, when she left: the education she'd painstakingly acquired (while growing and caring for her family), and the skills she'd worked so hard to build, recognized with gilded plaques and certificates housed in thick frames. A fresh coat of paint would prime the walls for their next tenant, a blank slate on which to display his or her own set of accomplishments.

Now, the items on her to-do list had gone from the complex tasks necessary to manage multimillion-dollar programs—the ones that made her feel like a superhero, able to solve the problems no one else could—to learning the hospital laundry schedule inside and out to keep her husband comfortable in his own clothes. She was always first in line to use the machines, and always ready to share her detergent with another patient's family member who was working to become reconciled to a loved one's diagnosis.

She was struggling to let go of her career and accept the simple, sometimes grueling responsibilities of being a caregiver. Her guilt over the reality that this new role wasn't completely fulfilling for her grew and grew each day.

But all she knew was how to give it her all, and that's just what she did. She remained by her husband's side for the next seven months. She squashed that guilt as best she could by being the best caregiver she could be. Fluffing pillows, changing sheets and shirts, playing music, improving lighting, and moistening dry lips, she made her husband's room a sanctuary. Her business became healing; her husband's treatment and progress became her quarterly benchmarks.

* * *

The endless medical trials eventually proved successful. Health was finally on the horizon for the Woman's husband. The days seemed lighter, and for the first time in months, the Woman felt real relief. Without work waiting for her, it seemed the perfect time to get some real rest and recharge her batteries.

During a lull in the action one afternoon, while her husband was napping, the Woman stepped out to check her e-mail. She curled up in a sunny spot in one of the hospital's common areas, enjoying the warmth on her face. Among the check-ins from friends and family and the coupons and advertisements that piled up within the span of a few hours, one subject line caught her eye: "Spiritual Solutions, Answers to Life's Greatest Challenges." The Woman clicked on it without thinking.

It was a retreat. Four days in sunny California at a resort with beautiful grounds, daily meditation and yoga, and wholesome, delicious meals. It sounded ideal to her—a little respite from everything she'd been through. Perhaps she'd even get the opportunity to think through the challenges that lay ahead and begin the work of figuring out what to do next, now that her husband was on the mend. Then, a little further down the screen, she read, "This retreat is designed for women who wish to find themselves."

She almost deleted the e-mail right then and there. Finding herself? What a self-indulgent waste of time. And for women only? *I don't need to be a woman*, she thought. *I need to be successful.*

But after she closed her in-box, a strange feeling lingered that this was a message she was somehow meant to receive. She opened the e-mail again. An image she'd disregarded before appeared alongside the text. It was a mesmerizing series of geometric lines, all coming together to form a circle—a labyrinth.

She closed the e-mail again. Her husband would be waking up soon, and she wanted to be there when he did.

## Chapter Three

The Woman's husband was cleared for discharge! She had never been so happy about packing—this time to go home. As she folded the blankets, wrapped the cords around her lamps, and nestled the photographs she'd brought into layers of newspaper, she was acutely aware that if they left everything behind and returned with only themselves, that would be enough.

They settled into a new life at home: both of them there all the time. They prepared meals together, spent long afternoons playing Sequence, and took the country drive they usually reserved for weekends on a Thursday, just for the fun of it.

They were having a wonderful time, but the nagging sensation the Woman had felt all along—her regret over leaving her job to become a caretaker—stayed with her. She knew she needed a rest, as well as some space to determine her next steps. She wasn't sure what she wanted to do, but she had to figure it out, sooner than later.

The Woman had left the Spiritual Solutions retreat e-mail in her in-box. She just couldn't bring herself to delete it. Every day she opened it, gazing at the geometric shapes that composed the labyrinth, turning over in her mind the possibility of actually attending. Her husband was much better and adjusting well to life at home, and the retreat would be short—a handful of days. With a little time to collect herself, she was sure she would be a better caretaker for him, if nothing else.

When she brought up the possibility of attending a retreat in California, she did so hesitantly; she didn't want to get her hopes up.

But her husband responded enthusiastically—he thought it was a great idea for her to get away for a bit, to focus on herself after so much time by his bedside, not to mention the many years before that she'd devoted to her job. He'd be fine without her for a little while, he assured her. Plus, it wasn't like they didn't have cell service in California. She could check in on him whenever she wanted. And they had a community of friends and loved ones ready and willing to lend a hand.

With her husband's encouragement, the Woman finally convinced herself that she could justify the trip. That night, she reserved her slot and booked her flight. She would leave in a week. She felt excitement bubble up, the promise of a new adventure on the horizon.

The Woman began gathering her things for the retreat, pulling out her loose-fitting yoga clothes and carefully folding them into her suitcase, along with a couple of her favorite family photographs. She also brought a notebook so that she could capture the advice of the many esteemed speakers who would be presenting during the retreat, as well as a folder to collect any important handouts she might receive.

The day of her departure came quickly, and before she knew it, she was readying herself for the flight and kissing her husband goodbye.

On the plane, the Woman carefully reviewed the information that had come with her welcome packet. She wanted to make the most of her trip, so she made a list of the speakers she wanted to see during her downtime and noted the drop-in yoga and meditation classes she planned to attend, creating a little schedule to augment the retreat's prescribed offerings.

After she had finished planning out her time—6:00 a.m. to 9:00 p.m. each day—she closed her eyes to take a quick nap. The plane was already making its final descent.

* * *

The Woman arrived at the resort just as the sun was setting. The clouds were shot through with streaks of orange and purple, and they seemed to glow from within, the soft, gray-blue expanse of the sky a perfect backdrop for their brilliance. She made her way to her room, marveling at the height of the palm trees lining the paths, the pristine Spanish-style buildings, and the perfection that is California weather.

After settling into her room and taking a quick shower, she headed to the retreat's opening ceremony. The retreat center was a ten-minute walk from the resort's grounds. Along the pathway stood a series of fountains, each topped with a stone bowl holding blazing coals that glowed against the darkening sky.

The air was thick with the smell of orange blossoms, and the Woman couldn't help but approach the nearest flower and stick her face right into it. She inhaled deeply—the sweet, slightly zesty scent filling her nostrils, reenergizing her after a long day of travel. She sighed. *This is relaxation*, she thought. *I'm doing it! I feel better already.*

The Woman wasn't surprised to be one of the first people to arrive; she was always early. The room that would serve as her home base for the next week was set up with semicircular rows of floor pillows. The Woman took her place in the front left-hand corner, close enough to have a good view, but not right in the front row. Despite a professional life marked by speaking engagements and other public events, she was an introvert at heart, and as such, she knew this would be her seat for the duration.

Soon the room filled with the other retreat goers, all of them women, ready to find themselves. She almost rolled her eyes; she couldn't help it—she had been conditioned to think women-only activities were somewhat ridiculous. And even though she wanted to be there—even though she felt she needed this retreat in ways she couldn't even fully articulate—she hadn't gotten past her discomfort with the women-only premise. The Woman silently chided herself: she would be open to the session and what it had to offer.

For women only or not, she was sure she needed it.

The speakers took the stage, sharing a bit about what the women could expect during the week. They would form small groups, and each of them would ask the other members of her group for help addressing a challenge in her life.

*Just one?* The Woman thought, chuckling quietly, *Where do I start?* But she was hopeful that the sessions the speakers were running through, the additional opportunities for meditation and yoga, and the Ayurvedic spa treatments she could indulge in if she liked, would have her leaving rested and balanced, with a clear idea of what was next for her.

If she could just get some time with the retreat leader, to hug him and ask his advice, that alone might be enough. He was a well-known, prolific writer and speaker, and the owner of the center to boot. He was successful *and* centered. Maybe he had the benefit of being a man, but he certainly seemed to "have it all." If she could figure out his secrets, maybe she could achieve the same.

She left the first meeting optimistic that she would get what she was looking for out of this investment, and upon returning to her hotel room, she fell into a deep, dreamless sleep.

* * *

The Woman awoke before sunrise the next morning, filled a little canvas bag with essentials for her day, and walked to her yoga class—stopping to inhale the heady orange-blossom scent along the way.

During the day's first session, the women were to begin working on the challenges they wished to address in their little groups. The Woman introduced herself to the two strangers who were now sitting across from her.

She thought about what she'd like to tackle with the help of her group. A few options ran through her mind. She was eager to figure out what was next for her career-wise, but she didn't think she wanted to discuss it here; it felt like too much to get into, and she wasn't sure these women would understand where she was coming from. She had thought about getting her husband a pet; she had read about the healing power of animals—but was that really a challenge? She didn't think so.

Asking for their assistance in determining whether to renovate her kitchen would certainly be a cop-out. But before she could come up with the perfect problem, it was her turn to share.

"Well," she started, "I've been trying to write my husband's memoir," surprising herself with what had risen to the surface. She explained to the women about her husband's cancer, how she had started writing about his life after he first became ill, but hadn't been able to pick it up in years. She told them how he had just been sick again after thirteen years in remission, and how his illness had reminded her of how fleeting time can be.

She'd tried to help him with this task at first, but soon found herself avoiding it.

"Why do you think you're avoiding it?" one of the women asked.

"I want it to be perfect. I'm afraid I'll be a failure, that I won't do his story justice."

"You're already a failure," the other responded, matter-of-factly.

"Excuse me?" the Woman said, taken aback.

"You haven't written it," she replied. It was as simple as that.

* * *

The next day, as the Woman left a group session, she found herself straying from what had quickly become her regular path. Her attention was captured first by a bed of deep purple flowers, then by the lush foliage nearby, and then by the intricate tile patterns on a large mosaicked fountain—which led her farther and farther from her path.

She ran her hand across the shiny, deep-blue tiles, their color so rich she thought her fingertips might sink into them. She stroked the fat, juicy leaves of a plant she couldn't name, the emerald green fading to pale pink toward the stem. She continued walking, her attention flitting from one beautiful sight to the next.

Then the Woman felt the texture of the ground beneath her thin-soled sandals change. It wasn't the soft grass that she'd padded through to sniff the orange blossoms, nor was it the slick surface of the concrete she'd stepped across to get a closer look at the remarkable fountains that lined the grounds. This surface was composed of pebbles, which were bumpy beneath her feet. As she looked up, she realized the pebbles made a pattern—the same pattern she'd seen in the retreat e-mail. She was standing in front of the labyrinth.

Out of the corner of her eye, she saw movement—someone was approaching. As this person came closer, she saw that it was a woman slightly older than she was, with long gray hair flowing down her back, and a crinkly smile. She looked familiar. Had she seen her in the café during breakfast, or at one of the group's icebreakers? Did she know her from home, or even from work? Some of her West Coast colleagues had been a little more woo-woo than their East Coast counterparts. But the Woman couldn't place her.

"Hello," the older woman said, touching the Woman's shoulder.

"Hi, do I know you from somewhere?" she asked.

"I'm your guide," she said. "I'm here to support you while you're here. Would you like to walk the labyrinth?"

"Oh no," the Woman said. "I've gotten so distracted already. I really have to—"

"It won't take much time," the guide said gently, interrupting her. "Or rather, it will take just enough time."

The Woman raised her arm to check her watch, but then remembered she had stored it in the hotel safe, vowing to be less attached to time during her stay. She had no real excuse to demur. Hadn't she come here to do exactly this type of thing?

"Okay," she told her guide.

"Wonderful. Slip off your shoes. Feel the stones beneath your feet, the way the pattern takes shape."

The Woman removed her sandals, placing them side by side next to the mouth of the labyrinth. She looked at the pattern stretching out in front of her, evaluating the twists and turns, thinking about where they might lead.

"There is only one way in and one way out," the guide said, but the Woman didn't quite hear her. She was focused on the task at hand, her analytical brain working overtime, attempting to solve the labyrinth before she even took her first step.

## Chapter Four

The Woman continued studying the twists and turns before her, attempting to unfurl them in her mind—to visualize a direct path to the heart of the labyrinth—but she couldn't. There were too many lines and curves, and when she tried to trace them, they tangled before her eyes.

She felt herself growing irritated; she didn't want to begin without knowing where she was going. And she could feel the minutes slipping by. She had wanted to stop by the gift shop on the way back to her room, and now there was no way she could if she was to make it to the afternoon meditation session. She looked back at her guide. "How do I do this?"

"What do you mean?" her guide responded.

The Woman took a deep breath. She started to describe the labyrinth itself, the way the path seemed to disappear around the first bend, at least from where she was standing—she didn't know where she was headed. But then, she found herself going deeper, explaining a greater frustration.

"My whole life I have been conditioned to be successful. I was taught to be a fixer. To figure out how to solve each problem put in front of me faster than someone else, to be better than everyone else. If I take on the challenge of completing the labyrinth, I want to do it right. And to do it right, I have to know how to solve it. If I can't tell where I'm going, how can I solve it?" She felt a bit hysterical, and more than a little self conscious, having offered up so much information to a virtual stranger.

But her guide seemed unfazed. "You were born complete, happy, and perfect," she replied. "Do not look at your life as a problem to solve."

The woman thought about all her success-driven social conditioning, how she had done all the things she was supposed to do, ever since she was a little girl. She had tried to anticipate any potential issues—big or small, molehills or mountains—and do her very best to prevent them.

Still, she'd had a stroke, she had been fired, and her husband had battled cancer not once, but twice. And she was unfulfilled. Her drive, her perfectionism, her solutions-oriented approach hadn't helped her to avoid any of it.

The universe kept throwing her challenges—one after another after another. She had always stepped up to each one, faced it head on, done the right thing—or so she thought.

But maybe her reactions hadn't been right all along. Maybe she was missing something. Maybe she wasn't really listening to what the universe was trying to say.

And perhaps she couldn't solve the labyrinth just by looking at it.

Her guide was still smiling at her encouragingly. With hesitation, the Woman took her first step.

Apprehensive, she looked to her right, then to her left, past the outermost border of the labyrinth. All around her were other guests of the retreat center. She could hear their chatter, the strum of guitar strings from a musician nearby, the drumming accompanying a dance class somewhere in the distance. They walked in groups and alone, sat in meditation on yoga mats rolled out in the grass, and lay sprawled on their backs staring at the clouds. But when she closed her eyes, she imagined them all watching her, judging her, anticipating her next move.

She tried to shake off their imaginary gaze. She was here to work on herself, and so was everyone else. They were unconcerned with what she was doing. It was only the Woman and her guide and the ground beneath her feet.

The Woman peered across the expanse of the labyrinth, furrowing her brow as she attempted once again to track each turn, to take mental notes of what was ahead so she wouldn't get lost. She wasn't sure what time it was, but she could see the sun dipping below the tops of the palms.

If she still wanted to make it to meditation, and to dinner, and then to hear the evening speaker, she would have to hurry. If only she could see beyond the first quarter of the labyrinth, she could estimate just how long it would take. She found herself wondering how much time it took most people to complete the labyrinth, how quickly it had been done before. Of course, no one recorded these things, so there wasn't really a way to know.

For a moment the Woman imagined her replacement, sitting at her old work desk, and wondered whether he or she was doing a better job than she had, whether her former colleagues liked their new team member more than they liked her. She felt a wave of panic as her mind flitted to what she would do after she left this labyrinth, this place, and reentered the real world without being able to return to the stability of her work.

What would she do? She couldn't go on playing board games and taking weekday joy rides with her husband forever. Her mentor had given her the name of someone to call—a friend who was a consultant—if and when she was ready to reenter the workforce. Maybe she should contact him before she left the center.

The Woman felt her guide touch her shoulder, bringing her back to her body. "Release the conditioning of your childhood; you do not need a plan to take a step forward. Find joy in the unknown and you can do what you were meant to do, not what other people tell you to do. You do not need to know where the path leads."

The Woman's mind was still racing. In a quivering voice, she asked, "What if I take a step too soon, or too late? Maybe I don't know enough to do this."

Her guide smiled, "You don't realize it, but you already have what it takes to do what you are truly called to do. Trust your instincts to take the best next step."

The Woman inhaled deeply, the way she had practiced in her session that morning. She pushed away thoughts of work and life outside the center—outside the path in front of her. She focused all of her attention on the undulating lines and began to move forward.

At each twist and turn, she felt herself let go a little more. Her shoulders slid down, away from her ears. She relaxed her brow.

The sky was getting darker, fluorescent orange fading to indigo all around her. At first she could feel every wisp of cool air that came with the sun's retreat and looked up frequently, tracking the day's descent toward the horizon. But eventually, the swiftly falling darkness no longer fazed her. She was immersed in the whorls in front of her, working her way around the labyrinth's second quarter.

When she looked up, she noticed that many of the retreat center's guests had headed off in one direction or another—a lone yoga mat or circle of chairs the only indication that they had been there at all. She could see her guide on the periphery, still smiling, her hair shimmering in the dwindling light.

With each step, the Woman released a little more of her worry, her conditioning, and her struggle. After what seemed like forever, the Woman saw the curves get tighter—the turns come more swiftly.

Then the labyrinth opened like the petals of a flower. She had reached its center!

The Woman was momentarily delighted. She had done it, and without any real charting, without knowing what she was getting into before she entered, without logistical insights from her guide.

But almost immediately, her mind flitted to how much time she had just spent on this endeavor. It was dark now; dinner was probably nearing its end.

*I have to get out of here*, she thought. She had told her husband she would give him a call, sometime between her meal and the evening speaker. It was three hours later on the East Coast, and if she had any hope of connecting with him, she'd have to hurry. She didn't want him to think that she had forgotten about him, caught up in pursuing some quest for who knows what while he continued to recover at home. She turned around, looking for her exit route.

Her guide spoke to her once again from the sidelines. "Learn to love yourself and stop being guilt-ridden over the fact that you must be the most important thing on your list. You have arrived! Relish your accomplishments; you are doing great things."

*She's so right*, the Woman thought. *How thoughtless of me.* She had almost missed an opportunity for reflection, the very purpose of her being there. The Woman stopped. She stood very still at the center of the labyrinth, its petals stretching out in every direction. Her breathing slowed. She raised her arms above her head, reaching for the sky, as if for the very first time. Her body seemed to open and release, her fingers spindling outward, a warm pulsing energy flooding through her. She could feel joy swelling in her chest, filling her heart. She looked up. The cool moon shone on her face. A deep gratitude began to bubble up.

She was thankful for all that she'd been through: her work and its corresponding challenges, her daughter, her husband—his kindness, his wisdom, and of course, his health—all that she'd learned in life so far, the way the cool pebbles felt beneath her still bare feet. She felt her joy stretching the muscles of her cheeks into a grin, pulling at the corners of her eyes.

Her guide encouraged her, "Stop focusing on knowledge and start focusing on consciousness.

No one told you your job was to be in control. Dance with the flow of life; this is bliss."

"Oh gosh, I love to dance!" the Woman exclaimed. "But there's really no time for that now, I'm already so late. I must get my money's worth, and if I don't get in line early, I won't meet the special guest speaker. I'm probably going to miss dinner at this rate. And I'm sure someone will comment that I have been away too long. How do I get out?"

Her guide's cool, pleasant demeanor cracked just a bit with the Woman's response. For the first time, she shook her head, her smile fading from her face. "Stop focusing on lack and creating victimhood by telling yourself that there's not enough time or money. Stop worrying about being perfect! When you let go of how to get there, you arrive right where you need to be."

The Woman flashed back to her life outside the carefully crafted serenity of the retreat.

So many troubles had come her way. It didn't seem fair that one person could be given all these hurdles to overcome. "But," the Woman replied, "I've been through so much. I know what it's like to run out of time and resources and money. I lost my job just a few years ago. My husband has been very sick. I left my career behind to take care of him. I don't even know what I'm going to do when I leave here!"

Her guide nodded, her smile returning. "The bad situations give you the ability to mentor others. The universe uses challenges as a teaching tool, not as a form of punishment."

The Woman closed her eyes, thinking for a moment. "What if I don't overcome those challenges? What if I fail? What will people think of me?"

"Live life like no one is watching!" her guide exclaimed. "Take your mask off and realize that you are infinite—and then you can accomplish anything. Move from doing to being; let go of people's expectations. Invest in yourself to increase your authentic power. You can't be the best you until you invest in you. The most important person you'll ever meet is not a celebrity or a business leader. The most important person you'll ever meet is you."

Opening her eyes, the Woman looked around for her guide and found that she was gone.

Alone, without her guide, the Woman breathed deeply. She saw the sky above her, infinite and black, pricked through with tiny clusters of stars. She could hear the wind moving through the palms.

For the first time in a long time, she didn't feel tormented by success or outside influences—the need to jump immediately to the next thing. She was happy to be right where she was.

Suddenly, she felt her feet begin to move, pounding the pebbles to the rhythm of the drums she'd heard earlier. The beat coursed its way from her feet up through her knees and into her hips, which swung from side to side. Her arms joined in, then her shoulders. Her head bobbed in time.

This time, the twists and turns came swiftly. She didn't think about the next bend, or where the labyrinth would release her. Time had lost its meaning. She was dancing!

And she danced her way out.

# Chapter Five

After the labyrinth, the Woman felt *lighter*. There had been a real shift for her there, along those pebbled switchbacks. The next morning she was practically skipping to her session, more energized than she had ever been. The retreat grounds seemed even more beautiful than they had a day ago, if that was possible. The flaming bowls topping the fountains appeared to glow brighter. The Woman felt as if the sunrise were emanating from her own heart.

She sat rapt through her sessions, taking copious notes, and found herself truly opening up to the other women in her group. The Woman was now sure that this retreat was not a frivolous pursuit. She was invigorated. This was what she had been looking for.

The following day—the second-to-last day of her stay—her group was introduced to a guest speaker who would lead them on a life vision. It would be one of the final steps in tackling the issues they'd raised in their small groups, at least during their time at the center.

"You've all come here to address a challenge," he said. "Today, we're going to take a moment to think about what may happen when we leave, when those challenges are still with us, alongside the obstacles of real life—a world without unlimited yoga and eight kinds of sprouts." He smiled and added, "For most of us, at least."

The Woman laughed. She liked this speaker already.

He instructed them to get comfortable, and the Woman went about organizing her little square of real estate, fluffing her floor pillow, adjusting her water bottle and notebook so that they were aligned and within arm's reach. She sat down and crossed her legs in front of her, letting her shoulders slide away from her ears, breathing slowly in and out, as the speaker began to guide them. Her eyes fluttered closed with his cue.

"Now," he said, "focus in on your challenge. See it laid out in front of you." The woman pictured her computer—the glow of the screen, the constant blinking of the cursor on the blank pages of her husband's memoir almost taunting her. Then the pages began to scroll before her, one after another, on a loop.

"Imagine it's three days after you arrive home," he intoned. "You haven't picked up your challenge. How do you feel?"

The Woman saw herself settling in, jumping back into the routine she and her husband had created just a few weeks before. She felt the serenity that had come with long lunches spent together, the delight she took in the daily chores she never had time to do before.

All the while, though, the challenge buzzed in the background, the computer screen still lit. It called to her as she puttered around the kitchen.

But three days wasn't too bad; it would take a while to get back into the swing of things—it probably made sense to give herself a window of time before she picked *anything* up, let alone this daunting task.

The speaker interrupted her attempts to assuage her anxiety: "Now imagine it's been three months."

In her head, the buzz became a constant drone, like the sound of a vacuum cleaner running a room away—a nagging sensation that tugged at her as she kissed her husband good morning and made their eggs, as she straightened their bedroom and had coffee in town with friends—the ever-present feeling that she should be doing something else. The woman shifted on her cushion.

"Now," said the speaker, "It's been three years."

The Woman knew how the days and weeks eaten up by those day-to-day tasks could turn quickly into years; so many things had slipped by while she was busy saving the world. She remembered work projects sucking up evenings and weekends, rushing to recitals and drill practice, flashes of the time she'd spent doing her best to help her husband fight his illness, with endless blankets and books on healing and prayers. The events of the past blurred together before her still-closed eyes.

Now she saw time begin to whirr again, going forward this time. It slid by while she organized a closet, fixed a hinge on the screen door, and finished that kitchen renovation she had been considering for what seemed like forever.

But all through those menial tasks and the hum of everyday life, she saw her husband getting sicker—frail again and stooping, the way he had looked that morning in the café. She saw her days of puttering around her kitchen replaced yet again by days confined to a hospital room.

The spare time she had to write her husband's memoir was evaporating.

In her mind, he was fading fast, turning transparent as the days rushed by.

Her breath caught in her throat. She imagined her husband dying before she could finish.

The Woman felt waves of emotion flowing over her as she pictured opening the files, the hollow click of the mouse sounding without him shuffling around nearby. She felt the full weight of the failure the other woman had mentioned on the first day of the retreat. Tears were streaming down her cheeks. Surrounded by a hundred other women, she was totally alone.

"But what if—" the speaker intoned, "what if instead, you take on your challenge? Imagine greeting it at the doorway to your home upon your return, committing to it in real, tangible ways. What would happen if you chipped away at it gradually, rather than letting it overwhelm you?"

The Woman pictured herself sitting down in front of her computer screen on her first night back, her skin still tan from the California sun. She took a deep breath and began to type.

It didn't come all at once—there were fits and starts. Along the way she and her husband went to their favorite café and started an herb garden and worked together to document his beautiful, complicated, challenging life so far.

She pictured long evening chats, she typing away while he sat nearby with his eyes closed, thinking back over their years together, and before that, back to when he was a little boy.

In her mind's eye they leafed through photo albums of their children, their wedding, and her husband growing up. The plastic pages of the album showcased bright spots. There he was, young and handsome in his navy uniform, riding a two-wheeler for the first time, blowing out the candles on his fourth birthday cake, and as an infant wrapped in a pale blue blanket—wearing the grin she knew so well. She and her husband were making new memories as they paged through the old ones and wrote them all down.

Finally, they arrived in the present, in which her husband was enjoying his retirement and his good health. She was figuring out what to do next—and grateful for the challenge.

On the last page, the Woman typed, "To be continued . . ."

* * *

When the Woman opened her eyes, she was still crying, but she was not alone. All around her were others who had just taken their own journeys, their eyes misty or contemplative or awestruck. They too had had the opportunity to explore what the world might have in store for them if only they made the decision to attempt something that scared them.

The Woman had been afraid that she wouldn't be able to do her husband's story justice, but she knew for sure that her group-mate had been right: The only way she would surely fail was if she didn't attempt his memoir at all.

Then, the Woman had an idea. With a little extra time, she could develop an outline for the memoir—a scaffold, a structure for the book. She and her husband could fill in the details together. She would see about staying an extra day at the retreat center to map it all out.

When the session ended, she hurried to call her husband and tell him about her plan.

He agreed immediately. He told her how wonderful she sounded. "I can hear the joy in your voice," he said. "You sound like you did when you were starting a new project at work, only less stressed."

The Woman could hear that familiar grin over the phone, and it made her giddy. When they hung up, she headed to the front desk to book another night.

The next afternoon, the group closed its final session with now-familiar songs, promises to stay in touch, hugs, and a few tears. The Woman felt content as their time together came to an end, watching the women walk out the doors of the room where they had shared so many intense moments in just a handful of days, eager to resume their lives. She was sure that many of their journeys were just beginning.

Many of the retreat's other programs were also ending that day, and the next group of retreaters—who were there to delve into meditation or explore Ayurveda or deepen their relationships—wouldn't arrive until the following morning. With no special guest speaker to meet, and no familiar faces to greet at dinner, the Woman savored the quiet. She ate her evening meal in comfortable silence, contemplating the task in front of her as she gazed across the almost-empty grounds from her little table.

Across the way she could see a man doing the same, completely immersed in thought. She realized that he must have finished his course and decided to stay on for a bit, like her, to think through some issue or other. She remembered how she had worried that finding herself was a trivial, female concern. *We're all just trying to figure it out*, she thought to herself. She smiled when she caught his eye, and he nodded in return.

After a restful sleep, the Woman awoke early, feeling invigorated. With a mug of hot tea, a notepad, and a pencil in hand, she made her way out to a seat by one of the towering fountains. As the sun rose, she began writing, ideas flooding through her fingertips onto the page. For the first time in a long time, the Woman was on fire.

\* \* \*

The Woman finished packing her things. It was time to go, and she was ready. As she made her way down the main path one last time, she stopped to inhale the intoxicating orange-blossom scent.

She was confident that she had made significant headway, but she also felt something deeper than the ordinary sense of accomplishment she typically had when she made progress on a project. It was the sense that bliss was possible, that if she could find it in a moment as seemingly insignificant as sniffing a flower, she could capture it in her everyday life.

On her way out, the Woman visited the retreat center's gift shop, hoping to take a piece of her experience home with her. She chose a handful of crystals, a set of glass tubes filled with essential oils, and a bronze singing bowl. She would place them on a shelf in her little studio back home and use them whenever she needed a reminder of the retreat center's magic.

After boarding the plane, with the scent of lavender on her wrists and a crystal nestled in her palm, she fell into a deep, peaceful sleep.

# Chapter Six

$H$abits are patterns burnt into our minds. Habits are hard to break.

Soon after returning home, the Woman fell back into old habits.

It was lovely to see her husband again after almost a week away. He looked terrific—the color had returned to his cheeks and he had already gained a little weight. She could tell how happy he was to see her.

And it was wonderful to be back home, nestled in the mountains.

On the evening of her return, the Woman and her husband cooked dinner side by side, and she told him about some of what she had seen and done, trying to capture the scent of those orange blossoms with only her words.

She described the labyrinth, the guide who supported her through it, and how, on the way out, she felt better than she ever had—ready to embrace all the possibilities the world had to offer, rather than looking to fix anything and everything she deemed imperfect.

The Woman's husband was thrilled to hear about her progress. She had been able to get the break she needed, and hopefully she'd be able to apply the same mentality to her everyday life. To grant herself the same kindness she had always shown everyone else.

But almost as quickly as the lavender oil faded from her wrists, the Woman found herself wondering how she would solve the riddle of her life.

Would she go back to her corporate life or strike out on her own? She had been fantasizing about writing a book or launching a company to help others weather challenges like the ones she had faced.

What was her plan? Industry or independence?

No matter what she did, the daunting question of what to do with her future loomed, following her relentlessly everywhere she went—to the grocery store, to the café, and on long walks through the woods.

* * *

One afternoon, unable to focus on the tasks she planned to do that day, the Woman opened her journal from the retreat.

She turned to a series of notes she had written to her future self during one of her exercises.

*The simplest way to live your soul's purpose is through silence. Each day, one way to finding my way—one step at a time—is meditation.*

Meditation sounded like a good idea. The Woman took her notebook and headed to her little studio.

*Meditation is the simplest way to connect to my spirit and find my vibration, the energy that fuels our souls,* she had written.

*Be quiet to hear the shift.*

She closed the door to the studio softly behind her and settled into a comfortable position on the floor.

From her seat, she gazed out through the room's big picture window. She loved this view, the way the forest cradled her home in lush foliage, trees going back as far as she could see.

*Quickly release any resistance with grace, power, and ease.*

The Woman closed her eyes and tried to relax.

She began taking deep breaths, attempting to let go, but the thoughts continued to creep in. Her mind sprang to the laundry in the washer, needing to be transferred. To what she'd prepare for lunch. To the seemingly innumerable things she could be doing—including caring for her husband, who she guessed was sitting on the other side of the door, waiting to spend time with her.

And then to the fact that she still lacked a bigger-picture plan.

She didn't know what she would be doing with herself next week, let alone with her entire future. In her mind's eye she saw unpayable imaginary bills begin to stack up, one on top of another—a product of her irresponsibility.

She opened her eyes. Meditation had seemed simple at the retreat, but at home, the Woman kept running into a brick wall of guilt. Whenever she took the time to meditate, the limiting voice inside told her she was being selfish.

She countered it with conscious thought: *All relationships reflect the relationship we have with ourselves. I am because I am, not because of someone else. I must be me, not what others want, and nothing will stand in my way.*

Putting herself first was new to the Woman; she had built her life around being last. It was not as easy as flipping a switch. Breaking that habit was hard, but she knew that she could only be the best version of herself if she invested in her own well-being. *This is not selfish, this is self-care*, she reminded herself.

She lit some incense and took her seat again, closing her eyes. *Sometimes relaxation takes work*, she thought.

* * *

As the Woman worked through her issues with making time for herself, she continued to struggle with the matter of her future.

*Where do you start when you need to rebuild your identity?*

During the visioning exercise, she had seen the way limiting beliefs could cause people to become stuck, wandering around in circles until they finally gave up, exhausted.

When she considered her path, she found herself flip-flopping between returning to industry and building her own business.

She imagined returning to her old company—how good it would feel to do something she felt totally confident about, how easy it could be. They had told her on many occasions that they would be happy to take her back, should she ever change her mind. She knew that if she accepted the offer, within a few weeks it would be like she'd never left. And she knew exactly who she was in that environment—strong, powerful, smart, and valued.

But then her mind would flit to the notion of creating something of her own. The freedom inherent in such an undertaking was both thrilling and terrifying to imagine. But she couldn't quite picture herself in that role the way she could envision herself striding across the stage in a business suit, speaking to hundreds of professionals hungry for her knowledge and experience. And yet, she couldn't shake the idea.

Maybe, she thought, some insights from the people she trusted would help her figure out what to do. She shared her dilemma with her husband, with her friends over coffee, and with her old mentor. All their responses were virtually identical: They'd listen to her intently, and then shrug. They couldn't make the decision for her—it was up to her. What would make *her* happy?

Frustrated one day after yet another non-answer over lunch, the Woman headed to her studio. Though she didn't feel any less stuck, meditation had become a little easier, and now she found herself eagerly turning to it when she needed a boost.

When she closed her eyes and attempted to clear her mind, both options hovered before her. She turned them each over, analyzing them as she always did. If she could just resolve this question—if she could figure out what to do with her life—then she would know where to place her energy. She could finally dive in headfirst.

Then she heard the voice of her guide, faint, as if she were calling from just outside the window.

*The world is full of problems,* the guide intoned, *but life is not one of them.*

Business is built on solving problems. The concept of success—at least as she had always defined it—required that there be problems to solve in the first place.

But this was not about arriving at the right solution. This was about transformation.

Then her guide's voice became her own: *You are reconstructing your journey; trust the horizon of your life.*

Instead of struggling to make a determination, she let her mind wander. When she pictured building a business or writing a book, she felt her pulse thrum with possibility.

Maybe she'd had the answer all along. Maybe it was less of an answer and more of a feeling. And maybe that was enough.

\* \* \*

The Woman had known she needed to have a conversation with someone, but she never realized that the conversation partner she needed was herself. She remembered something she had written in her journal, and now she picked it up and fumbled for the page.

*If you are looking for the answers to any situation, the knowingness you need to transform your life, just look in the mirror. The*

Woman got up and peered into the little mirror mounted on the wall.

She knew what she wanted to do. Now she just had to convince herself that she could do it.

*Asking empowering questions will give you guidance on the universe's idea for your life,* her journal urged. *This is how you transform.*

The Woman began a simple conversation with herself.

She asked herself three questions:

*Who am I?*

*Am I on the right path?*

*What do I believe about myself?*

When she asked herself who she was, she was not questioning her current role in life, or even the professional title she'd eventually take on. It was deeper.

She was inquiring as to who she was on a spiritual level. What did she stand for? What was the essence of her existence?

*What do I believe about myself?* She found herself saddened by the responses her mind produced when she asked that question. She had so much self-doubt.

Despite her excitement about starting something new, that limiting voice urged her to stay in her comfort zone—it was so safe, simple, and low-risk. And besides, what if she couldn't hack it as an entrepreneur?

Sure, she was organized, but did she really have what it took to strike out on her own?

She could feel the negative thoughts building up, limiting her courage to break free and try new things. One of the retreat speakers had warned that negative self-talk erodes our vibration—the energy necessary to do the work we're here to do. The barrage of responses proved her self-talk needed to change. The Woman knew she had to shift. She had to be kinder to herself.

She had been successful in industry, but she didn't want to work toward someone else's agenda anymore. Now she had to tell herself that she didn't have to. *She* was the priority. She herself was the journey.

Industry had taught her how to design and build and make change happen. She had to remind herself that she still had all of those skills. She could deploy them as she wished.

She knew it was worth it to invest in herself, but she had to remind herself of that also. And that finding herself was going to take a while, and that, too, was okay.

Once a week, she asked herself those same three questions: *Who am I? Am I on the right path? What do I believe about myself?* And as time went by, the Woman began to understand who she was on the inside. She explored and expanded her beliefs about her path—and her potential. She was beginning to truly believe in herself. Finally, the Woman had the courage and strength to transform her life.

*To manifest anything in life, set the intention or desire, focus your attention, your energy, and then let go—believe, and you will receive,* she had written. Now she was ready to do it.

\* \* \*

One morning, the Woman awoke to find her husband's side of the bed empty.

*That's strange,* she thought. Her pulse quickened, worrying that perhaps he had gotten up in the middle of the night in need of something and fallen.

*Why didn't he wake me,* she wondered nervously as she clambered out of bed. He wasn't in the bathroom, or in the guest bedroom, where he would read occasionally when he couldn't sleep. She paused at the top of the stairs, listening for him, and reached down to pet one of the cats circling her legs. "Honey?" she called. No response.

In the kitchen, the previous night's dishes had been done and were drying in the rack. There was fresh coffee in the pot and a note on the counter, next to her favorite mug.

*Out of milk. Ran to the store. Be right back!* XOXO, her husband had scrawled.

Her pulse finally began to slow. Her husband had done all that? She marveled at how his energy had returned.

The Woman took a deep breath. She palmed the note and walked toward the front door.

When she stepped onto the front lawn, she was barefoot. The grass was still beaded in dew. A layer of clouds had settled over the mountains during the night, and they were a beautiful silvery purple in the low light of the morning.

She looked at the note again. On the back, her husband had drawn the two of them—stick figures with familiar hair—surrounded by coffee mugs and hearts. She laughed.

*What a glorious* day, the Woman thought. *I feel different. I feel free.* She wasn't just a caregiver anymore; she was a partner. And she was laughing again.

\* \* \*

The Woman headed back inside, picked up her journal, and settled onto the couch. She began writing. *Happiness is not an external object; it's an internal anchor that no one can uproot once you have grounded yourself in your soul's purpose—and once you have let go of your guilt. When you give yourself the permission to be you, you are in control.*

*Go deep into the source of spirit to connect with your authentic self—that is where you find your vibration, your vibe. Do not reduce yourself to the old you of the past.*

*Pain pushes us until we can no longer endure the old ways. That is the moment when vision pulls us. During that pain, let go, listen, and trust your instincts. You only find yourself in the silence. Let bliss be your guide. That's the secret.*

*Be aware, live in conscious awareness, and when you feel bliss, repeat. Choice is a function of awareness. Without expanded awareness, choice remains restricted to the old conditioning. But when you become consciously aware, you are empowered to create a reality of your choosing. When you live your wholeness, you become complete.*

It was then that the Woman realized how drastically her definition of success had changed. So much of what she'd believed was important had dissolved.

All that remained was love.

# Chapter Seven

*L*ife began to expand for the Woman.

She finally believed her ideas had promise, and her positive self-talk was contributing to her growth and transformation.

As a result, orange-blossom-like moments began to spring up every day—especially when it came to her potential. She began scribbling ideas about who she was and what she could accomplish onto self-stick notes and putting them up around her studio.

Her daily practice of sitting in silence had also given her new insight into the kind of future she wanted to create. She now knew she wanted to start with her book.

She had built a strong outline for the memoir during the retreat, and now she started filling in the rest, complementing her time spent meditating with hours dedicated to writing. She built her own ritual around the process, slipping off her shoes, sitting at her desk, and working diligently to flesh out her husband's story.

She thought back to the fateful day of his diagnosis, how the symptoms he'd thought were just a complication of his diabetes were actually signs of leukemia—a form so aggressive that they left the doctor's office on Friday with plans to begin treatment on the following Monday. They were instructed to celebrate that Thanksgiving as if it were their last.

During his illness, the Woman and her husband looked for stories from those who had been through what they were facing, but they found very few resources—only a very brief account from a man named Tom, who had gotten sick, gotten better, and gone back to work. The Woman wanted to share their story so that others searching for community or coping strategies or comfort would know they weren't alone.

She had been talking about writing a book for years, but the need to get it perfect always held her back. After the retreat and the visioning exercise, she knew that she couldn't let perfectionism hold her back; she just needed to get it out there.

Sometimes her husband sat by her side as she wrote, adding his perspective. Other times, she worked alone late into the night, fueled by her desire to give life to this narrative, and to support those facing their own seemingly insurmountable challenges.

Within the year, the Woman had made something she was proud of. Even better, she had found a publisher—she would be able to share it with the world.

* * *

The Woman got word that her book was ready to go. It was time to plan for the launch. The publisher had offered her a couple of options, but she wanted to do it somewhere she felt comfortable, a friendly environment where she knew her most personal project to date would be well received.

As she sat at her desk, considering what her ideal launch might look like, an e-mail arrived in her in-box. The retreat center was hosting a conference on healing—complete with a book event featuring new works on the subject!

She continued to scan the information. Noting the date, she realized that she and her husband would already be in California at that time, visiting his sister.

It seemed like serendipity: What better place to launch her book than the one where she had made so much progress toward this very project, and toward her own healing? She would be surrounded by the people who had helped set her on her path. She considered all the new connections she could make with people working in the healing arts—connections that could probably help her spread her book's message. Perhaps most important, it would feel safe.

The event itself began to take shape in her mind. The Woman pictured herself walking hand in hand with her husband along the grounds of the retreat center, showing him the deep blue of the fountain tiles and the magnificence of the glowing coals against the sky, and even leading him through the labyrinth where she had achieved her very first breakthroughs. She imagined arriving at the center's main building and greeting the retreat staff at the event—the warmth of their hugs, and how good it would feel to share her book for the first time with a roomful of people who were sure to affirm her. She could even sign copies in the little gift shop, amid the smell of lavender, the tinkle of chimes, and the books of hundreds of established, successful wellness authors.

The Woman pitched the plan to her husband a few days later, and he quickly approved; it lined right up with their travel schedule, and he was looking forward to visiting this place he had heard so much about.

Now that she'd found the right venue, all she had to do was arrange it.

Sitting in her studio, a hot cup of coffee by her side, the Woman carefully composed an e-mail to the event's organizer. She was excited to share the news that she had finally finished the book, and to add her name to the roster of readers.

Within half an hour, she had a response. The woman could feel her nerves percolating as she clicked on the little envelope icon.

"Oh honey, I'm so sorry," the organizer had written back. "We're all booked up."

"Oh, that's all right," the Woman said to no one in particular, trying to dislodge the newly formed lump in her throat. She stared out the window of her studio, watching the wind move through the trees.

As she closed the e-mail, she realized just how much she had hung her hopes on this one opportunity. She had considered it to be a guarantee, and now it was hard to imagine launching anywhere else.

Disappointment flooded in. *If only that one thing had come through*, she thought to herself, *everything would've been perfect.*

This kink in her plan felt like a punishment for all kinds of missteps. Why hadn't she contacted the center earlier? Or even finished her book sooner? If only she had been more disciplined.

All those limiting beliefs started rushing back, and her mind began to swell with them like a river rising during the rainy season. She worried about how her book would be received, now that she couldn't introduce it in one of the safest spaces she knew. She imagined ridicule from critics, picturing a group of faceless strangers tearing it apart.

And what would that mean for her career as a whole? She was sure now that she didn't have the skills to succeed in this realm. How silly of her to think that she did!

Failure was one of the Woman's biggest fears. She had been able to stave it off for so many years, but she felt as if she had finally come face to face with it. She was

paralyzed by the prospect of defeat, or even the unknown—something far outside her comfort zone—and she had no idea what she would do next.

* * *

"I've started to book hotels for our trip," her husband told her during dinner that evening. "How many nights should I reserve at the retreat center? Should we get a room for my sister as well? I'm sure she'd love to come. . . ." he trailed off, noticing how her body language had changed.

The Woman was looking down at her plate. "They don't have any room for me," she said, unable to hide her dismay. Then all of her anxieties bounded out, one after another after another.

She told her husband about all the mistakes she was sure she was making. If she couldn't even launch her book properly, how could she navigate a whole creative career?

How foolish she had been to pursue such a ridiculous dream!

"What am I even doing?" she finished, tears rolling down her cheeks.

Her husband stood up and came around to the Woman's seat, resting his hands on her shoulders. "What *are* you doing?" he said. "You are a published author! Do you know how many people dream of being published? You have accomplished so much, honey! Be proud of yourself—you are doing great things!"

When she looked up at him, he was smiling encouragingly. She knew without a doubt that he believed in her. And she remembered that, all these months, she had been working to grow her belief in herself. *He's right*, the Woman thought. Her fear had washed away the reality of her accomplishments in a matter of minutes and replaced them with a bottomless pit of worries. But she knew those accomplishments were still there and that the pit existed only in her mind.

*I need to face my fears. I need to stop feeling helpless and start looking forward, even if I don't know exactly where I'm headed.* This was just another challenge; it wasn't a punishment. It was a way to learn more about herself and all that the world had to offer.

The retreat seemed so long ago now, and despite her best efforts, she found it hard to hold on to these concepts outside of the reassuring setting of the center, where her biggest challenge was choosing between afternoon yoga and meditation. It was part of why she wanted to go back so desperately. But she remembered what her guide had told her, that she couldn't be her best until she invested in herself. She knew that sometimes such an investment might require quashing some of her fears in order to take a leap of faith.

But her guide's words had stayed with her, and as she cleared the dishes from the table, she heard the wise woman's voice: "The most important person you'll ever meet is not a celebrity or a business leader. The most important person you'll ever meet is *you*."

Now it was up to her to take a chance. She needed to continue to let go of perfection, believe in her potential, and venture into the unknown.

\* \* \*

The Woman knew the definition of perfection that she had been raised with was completely outdated. When she was a child, her father had impressed upon his daughter that for a woman, there were two routes to success: Miss America or Suzy Homemaker.

Of course, times had changed; there were now as many definitions of *perfect* as there were women in the world. But childhood conditioning is hard to shake. Despite her many accomplishments in realms far removed from beauty pageants or domestic excellence, the Woman was still dogged by her father's image of the feminine ideal. It was hard for her to believe in her success, no matter how much she'd already achieved, and even more so when her goals didn't fit into a traditional pink box.

Her book project—and an unconventional professional life that it might evoke—was no different; she was constantly questioning its validity.

But the Woman knew that if she didn't address her fears—all of them—no matter how many retreats she attended, no matter how many notes she took, and no matter how many times she reread them, she would never realize her path.

While she wouldn't have the safety net of the retreat center to usher her work into the public sphere, she did have years of experience that she could apply here, too. She had creativity in spades. And more important, she believed in the value of what she was doing and its potential to help others.

* * *

As she continued to expand her awareness, another challenge concerning power and place arose for the Woman, this time in her personal life.

The Woman's father was turning ninety, and she had the honor of planning and hosting his birthday party. This responsibility was not a stretch for her—she was well known in many circles for her ability to put together the perfect event for any occasion. And this one would be particularly simple: Her father delighted in being the center of the attention, so doing something he'd love was as easy as inviting his many friends from his social club.

Although the Woman's mother had passed away a few years earlier, her father was still healthy and full of life, and she wanted to throw him a celebration that would reflect the joy of this milestone. The Woman thrilled in the process of shopping for party décor, ordering food, and choosing the perfect cake to mark her father's special day. On the morning of the party, she loaded up her car. She was excited to celebrate with friends and family and to show him all she'd put together to make his birthday the best one yet.

The familiar landscape of her hometown greeted her as she pulled off the highway. She took a series of winding roads she knew like the back of her hand, the flutter of pre-party butterflies growing as she approached.

In her head, she ran through mental lists of supplies she'd brought, how she'd arrange them, and any last-minute errands that needed to be run before guests arrived—confident that it would all go off without a hitch. Finally, she parked in the driveway of the house where she'd grown up.

"Hi Daddy-o," she said, as she came through the front door, arms laden with bags and boxes.

"Hi honey," he said, greeting her with a warm embrace.

"Let me show you what I brought," the Woman said, heading into the kitchen. "I can't wait!"

She placed her bags on the counter began listing tasks yet to be completed.

"Well you know," he said, "today's the lake festival. I thought we could head over there for lunch first."

She found herself nodding along with his plan, despite all that she had left to do. Despite the fact that she was tired—she had been driving for hours—and she had hoped to have time to rest before the party began. And she knew it would be blazing hot by the lake at this time of year. Still, she reached for her keys on her counter, thinking about how she might be able to make it to the store on the way back if she drove just a little bit over the speed limit. Maybe a quick shower would be just rejuvenating enough.

But now that the Woman was more consciously aware of her behavior, she realized what she was doing. Part of her deep-rooted conditioning was to be a people pleaser, especially here, in the place where the conditioning had first been instilled.

Each time she returned home, she let go of her personal power, relinquishing it to the man who had always been the primary authority figure in her life. Whenever she walked through those doors, she was a little girl again, dutifully completing her chores to her father's specifications.

But this wasn't about her father. This was about her, and the role she chose to play. It was up to her to make the change. She needed to practice being her own person.

"Dad," she began, "I think I should go pick up the food instead—I don't want to be rushed. And it would be great to take a quick nap before your party, so I'm refreshed and ready to entertain!"

"Alright," he said, shrugging. "That sounds good. See you in a bit."

*Huh*, she thought. His reaction was not at all what she had expected. He wasn't angry or annoyed. He didn't convince her to come along anyway. He just headed out—off to get his favorite ribs.

The party was a huge success. The Woman was able to get everything she needed and even sneak in some rest. Her father had a wonderful time, and so did everyone in attendance. They admired the cake and the decorations, and exclaimed over and over how happy her father looked to be celebrating with friends and family by his side.

Driving home early the next morning, the Woman felt grateful for the small challenge she had faced with her father. She had realized that she had a choice. And the outcome she feared—that her father would be angry with her, or that she would disappoint him—turned out to be just that: a fear. And one that quickly dissipated when she had the courage to be honest.

It made her reflect on how her expectations of others had the potential to hold her back. She thought about how every challenge she had faced had taught her something and helped her to circle closer to her center. And in this moment, she could see the commonality in all of them: she always had a choice; she was never as stuck as she thought she was.

\* \* \*

The Woman began to review the launch ideas from her publisher. They suggested that she participate in their upcoming "I Can Do It" conference in New York City. *That could work*, the Woman thought to herself. Attendees would pay the cost of admission and then have access to all the authors featured, as well as free copies of their books. While it might not have been what she'd envisioned, it would certainly give her plenty of exposure.

She decided that even though it didn't necessarily feel *perfect*, she would do it. Life is not a straight line from point A to point B. It's the detours along the way that make it a journey. The Woman was determined to shed her fears and her thoughts about how things should or shouldn't be and embrace the unexpected with wonder. Her husband and daughter would go with her, and she was grateful for their support.

\* \* \*

The Woman arrived at the conference unsure of what to expect. She linked arms with her husband and her daughter as they took in the enormity of the space, mostly empty in the early morning hours. As she waited on line with the other authors to claim her name tag, the woman behind her struck up a conversation. "What's your book about?" she asked.

"Oh," the Woman replied, caught off guard, "It's about being positive in the face of adversity."

"That's wonderful!" the other woman responded, and promptly began talking about her own trials and tribulations in the realm of adversity.

*Interesting*, the Woman thought. This experience was different from any that she'd had before, and it was thrilling.

Soon another author approached her and began a similar conversation. "What's your book about?" she asked. "Can I see it?"

The Woman hadn't even thought to carry a copy around with her. *I've got so much to learn*, she thought. But it didn't deter the author she was speaking with: upon being told the subject of the Woman's book, she immediately launched into a rundown of her own struggles.

The Woman was elated. She was eliciting incredible reactions from strangers—just the kind she wanted, though she hadn't realized it before. And even though she didn't know exactly how to be in this environment, or what it would hold for her, she felt comfortable here.

The doors opened to the public and before she knew it, the line of people waiting to meet her and pick up a copy of her book stretched back as far as she could see. They would tell her stories about themselves and their own challenges, or about family and friends who had recently been diagnosed—about how her book was just what they needed. The Woman hugged each and every one of them.

"Excuse me, ma'am," a man said, approaching the Woman with a large camera. We're making a video for the conference. Would you like to participate?"

"Sure!" she said. She was barefoot—just as she was when she wrote—wearing a soft, swaying sweater dress. She couldn't help but giggle as they interviewed her about her book and the experience of being at the conference. She could say in all honesty that it had been magical.

The Woman had let go of her conception of how she would accomplish her goals, and when she did, what she tapped into far surpassed anything she could've imagined. She found that what she wanted wasn't something she could've pictured. It wasn't about tangible items; it was about a *feeling*. It was not the prestigious title, the big house, the three cars—all the stuff we typically imagine. It was anything that could evoke the feeling:

a favorite chair, a warm scarf, the cat at her feet. A book launch in an unfamiliar space, surrounded by strangers who embraced her with open arms.

* * *

The Woman's daughter was now grown. Even though she still lived nearby, she had matured into her own person with her own life and navy career. She was a busy woman, and spending time with her in New York was a treat. As the end of the day neared, the Woman's daughter asked if they could talk, and she immediately agreed to slip away and chat.

They headed to a coffee shop nearby and sat at a little table. "I'm thrilled with how things are going!" the Woman said, bubbling over with energy from the conference.

"That's amazing, Mom," her daughter said, pausing for a moment. "That's actually part of what I wanted to talk to you about. I know how much you're enjoying the stuff you're doing with your book and retirement and all that. But I have to tell you that I'm pretty upset with you."

The Woman was shocked. She had no idea that any part of this journey had disappointed her daughter. "What?" she asked. "What do you mean?"

"Well," her daughter began, "You've always been an authoritative voice for women in business. A voice that I've always listened to. You've helped me face my fears and realize that I have a choice. You've helped me navigate so much of my life and career.

"I remember being on the ship and hearing all the other sailors' crazy stories. I never had anything to add because you told me I could never do anything wrong if I wanted to be a senator. I've always been really proud of that, actually." She laughed.

"I grew up listening to you mentor people on the phone," she continued, "watching you help them at conferences. I loved hearing you talk about how things had turned out when you'd given someone advice about what to do next. There is no one else like you out there. You've already changed people's lives, whether you know it or not.

"And now that you're retired from industry, it's like you took your voice and put it in a box on the shelf—like you don't need it anymore. Why did you put your voice away? Why can't it have a place in what you're doing now?"

The woman was quiet, thinking about all her daughter had said. In that moment, she realized she had been playing it safe, hiding behind her fears, taking the easy route. While she had been able to focus on her book and produce something that made her proud, she had been hesitant to really delve into the question of her path in life. Doing nothing— or even doing something safe—felt easier than looking at the bigger picture, figuring out her purpose in life.

She took a deep breath. "Thank you, baby girl. Thanks for telling me that. I think you're right."

The Woman had thought her work was already done, but there was actually much more to do. She had to find the courage to transform into the person she was sent here to be, in all her glory. That meant figuring out what she *really* loved doing—the next step toward finding her path, her soul's purpose.

*Surrendering to the flow of life*, the Woman thought, *will lead to the discovery of treasures that are only found during the time of transition.*

# Chapter Eight

The seasons had changed once again. It was autumn, and the Woman felt she was running out of time. It had been over a year since she'd attended the retreat, and months since the book launch, and she had not yet figured out how to move her life forward.

As she prepared for bed one evening, hanging the jeans she had worn that day in her closet, she felt something in the one of her pockets—a lump. She pulled out a square of paper and unfolded it. It was the note her friend had given her long ago:

*All the success in the world cannot satisfy divine discontent. You are looking for something more.*

She had thought she'd found what she was looking for, but now more than ever, she knew she was still searching. With each step she took, she was testing and tweaking the hypothesis of her future—seeing whether what she'd figured out really worked the way she'd imagined it would. It seemed as if that hypothesis was an ever-moving target.

She had figured that transformation would take time . . . but she hadn't expected it to take *this* long.

\* \* \*

The Woman was sure she wanted to help people through her work, but the question of how exactly she would do that remained. She could see herself sharing her experience with cancer patients and their families, providing reassurance and hope. She thought about developing workshops for nurses, using her time spent in hospitals as a framework to help them take better care of others *and* themselves.

She thought about focusing on children, writing books that would instill in them the kind of confidence she wished she'd had growing up. Or maybe she'd create something for parents instead—a guide to raising strong, happy kids.

The Woman began developing varied and elaborate business plans for each of her possible futures. Soon, strands of color-coordinated self-stick notes detailing potential strategies stretched across her studio walls. Each day she came up with a new idea or a catchy slogan, jotted it down, and stuck it up on one of the few remaining blank spaces in her cocoon of creativity. She drew logos, made posters, and visualized merchandise. Eventually, she lost track of which way was up.

The Woman had gone off the edge. She was stuck in a creative do-loop, second-guessing everything she came up with, constantly wondering if *this* was the idea that would make it.

Her failure to make a decision got her thinking. True creativity comes from uncertainty, the ultimate quantum idea. She had no shortage of uncertainty—that was for sure. If she wanted to bring any of her ideas to fruition, however, she would have to get her uncertainty under control.

She thought back to its origins in her social conditioning. The Woman's father had been a powerful influence in her life. He had been in the navy, and she'd grown up playing in his old uniform, donning his Cracker Jack top and pretending to be a sailor. She'd wanted so badly to secure his approval.

Knowing that a big title and a salary to match would impress her father, she began chasing after the kind of career he would be proud of. She ascended the professional ladder, acquiring more education, more money, more clout. No matter what she did, however, she never felt it was enough.

As she sat in her studio reflecting on the career she had pursued and the station she had risen to in industry, she realized whose path she had been chasing all that time: that of a white male. That's who made a corporate salary. That's who embodied the brand of success she had striven to achieve.

And she did it; she became the white male that industry wanted to invest in, racking up degrees and dollars and titles. She checked these boxes while wearing a wardrobe consisting of simple, professional pieces in sensible shades of black, gray, and navy so as not to attract too much attention as she worked her way to the top. She had done so much to prove that she was worthy, though she never quite believed it.

And even though she now recognized the social conditioning that had led to this life of tormented success, understood its impact, and tried to let it go, she was still stuck.

If her old life was fueled by what were widely considered to be the masculine energies of competition and accomplishment—climbing the corporate ladder—then this new life was ruled by a gentler feminine energy, ultracreative and collaborative. She had driven herself to the opposite extreme: this endless creative do-loop of self-stick notes and uncertainty.

Her daughter had been right about her business side. It had value too, and incorporating that skill set might help her break free. But she didn't know how to balance the aggressive left-brain side that drove analytical, rational thinking with the imaginative right-brain side fueling her instinct, emotion, and creativity.

*How will I be remembered?* she found herself asking, frustrated by all this wandering. *Why am I here? Why does any of this matter?*

Then a thought occurred to her: *She was the one who had discovered her husband's illness.*

It had taken skill and sense from both sides of her brain: the instinct that something was wrong, the capacity for analysis necessary to recognize the change in his appearance, and the determination to take action as soon as possible. And during those long days at the hospital, she had used her emotional intelligence to soften the experience of treatment for them both. More than anything, she was struck by the fact that she'd discovered it by paying attention, by quieting both sides of her brain long enough to really see it.

Returning to her journal, she read: *It's not the grand things we do that are important. Rather, it's the small meaningful moments that matter.*

The moment when she recognized the signs of her husband's illness was minuscule: the half second of a hug. It was a blip—a sight that could have easily gone unseen if she hadn't muted the buzz of her mind. She wasn't a medical doctor. She didn't have a road map of how to get to her husband's diagnosis. She had just *felt it*. And she'd listened.

She had already tapped into a hybrid of traditionally masculine and feminine traits. She could do it again as she forged her path. Maybe she had to reach the amplitude of the creative pendulum before she could swing back and finally rest in a balance that would allow her to pick something that brought her joy. Then she could stop the wandering, focus on that something, and deliver.

But first she would have to let go of how to get there, especially since she didn't know exactly where she was going.

\* \* \*

The Woman was in her studio again, diagramming her latest idea. The radio buzzed in the background, and she would catch a word or phrase here and there as she worked.

". . . exciting contest for you!" the Woman heard. She stopped what she was doing.

"We're looking for stories about overcoming challenges. The most compelling ones will be shared on this program."

What if *this* was her big break—an opportunity to help others through storytelling, and a big public platform from which to do it? Perhaps it would initiate a series of speaking engagements and lead the Woman to the audience she was looking for.

She jotted down the contest entry details: She would have to record a video of herself and send it in to the radio station. The Woman liked this new plan, and she liked it even more when her daughter agreed to come over that weekend and help her tape her entry.

On recording day, she put on her favorite blue sweater dress—the same one she wore for her book launch in New York—to boost her confidence and her mood. She cleaned out an area of her studio and set her favorite chair there. When the Woman's daughter arrived, they got right to work.

Three takes in, the Woman was getting nervous. She couldn't seem to get it right. She would start out confidently, and then somewhere along the way, she would stumble and get flustered.

*Okay*, she told herself, *just relax and focus. Breathe.* She resettled herself in her chair, looked right at her daughter, and calmly told her story. This time, the words just came to her, as if from thin air. This version was clear and poignant.

The Woman could barely contain her excitement. "That was perfect!" she said. "I think we've got it!"

"Let's try it one more time," her daughter said.

"But why? I thought it was great! Didn't you?"

"Yes," her daughter slowly answered. "But I forgot to press *record*."

Instead of getting upset that the best version of her story hadn't been captured, the Woman laughed. *Wasn't this the way life worked?* She was in the moment, enjoying the time she was spending with her daughter. "That's okay," she said. "We'll just try it again."

* * *

Much like meditation, letting go took practice. When the Woman found out a few weeks later that her entry hadn't been chosen, it was hard not to feel defeated. She had put herself out there and it hadn't worked out.

That familiar feeling of failure attempted to sneak in, but she was proud that she had tried.

*You don't know what's behind a particular door until you open it,* she told herself, *and this door just wasn't yours.* And in the process of trying, she'd had fun. She'd spent time with her daughter. She'd worked on telling her story effectively on film. The Woman smiled as she considered what she had learned just within the context of this small effort.

*Remember,* the Woman told herself, *every moment is just energy. When you are low, focus on gratitude. Let the energy lift you up, let the joy return. Release the moment and move on.*

The Woman's husband had built her a Zen deck outside, and it had become her sanctuary in moments like this one. Autumn had given way to winter particularly quickly that year, and she could see her breath as she stepped onto the deck. The thermometer informed her that it was twenty-five degrees.

She rubbed her palms together as she looked off to the east. The creek on their property wasn't completely frozen; she could hear it running in the distance. She loved it out here, but she'd need to move a lot more if she was going to stick around for more than a few seconds.

Without thinking too much about it, the Woman started to dance. As she moved, she felt the weight of her worries falling away. Her energy—her vibration—was rising.

Dancing had always been a joyful experience for her, ever since she was a little girl. She had taken classes from the time she was four all the way through high school. As an adult, however, she had left it behind—until she danced her way out of the labyrinth.

Weddings were the one exception. At a wedding she felt as if she had permission to dance, and so, at these events of organized joy, among grandparents and cousins and friends, she would take her place on the dance floor, throw her head back, and put her whole body into it.

She didn't need permission anymore. Whenever she needed to, she could shift her emotional state through blissful, rhythmic movement. She had found her vibe. Like meditation or a mind-clearing walk, dance was her tool.

When she felt herself begin to get caught up in too much planning, the Woman stopped her scribbling, put on some music, and began to dance. She soon found other ways to raise her vibration. She could walk the half mile to her mailbox, spying wild turkeys flying overhead or the occasional black bear making its way down the mountain, and feel grateful for the remarkable setting in which she lived. Or she could take a moment to leave her studio and wrap her arms around her husband while he read a book or worked on a crossword puzzle, basking in the glow of his steady, unconditional love and support.

These snippets of space and time brought her joy. They also helped her expand her awareness, reminding her that success was not external confirmation; it was internal transformation.

* * *

The Woman awoke early one morning. It was still dark outside, and the stars were blinking in the vast fabric of the sky. Her husband was snoring lightly beside her. She threw on some leggings and a sweatshirt and went downstairs to put on a pot of coffee.

The house was silent, dark except for the kitchen light. She filled her travel mug, pulled on her coat, and slipped outside for a walk. It had snowed the night before, and the air was bracingly cold. She took a road that hemmed the woods, listening to the sounds of night transitioning into morning—birds chirping, the rustle of creatures underfoot and in the trees. Leaves and twigs from the forest littered the road in front of her. The wind was strong, prickling against her cheeks and whistling through the branches above.

As she rounded a bend that traced the woods, she came upon a roadblock of sorts. One of the trees appeared to have split in half, the top of it lying all the way across the road.

*The wind is invisible*, she told herself, *yet you can see the product of its efforts: It can topple the tallest tree. Your power is the same. It's invisible within you, yet you can manifest it to change the world for the better—if you can create space for it.*

While working in industry, the Woman had worried that if she had been her true self, she would have blinded her colleagues with her light. Now she wasn't holding back; there was room for her to be herself, to find an energetic balance.

The seed of a plan began to crack open in the Woman's mind, delicate green shoots bursting through and spiraling outward, and she let it.

Creative thoughts melded with more practical considerations: What she would do, who it would be for, and how she would reach them. What her business might look like in a month's time, in a year, in five. But this plan was not hard and fast. While it had structure, it also had room for growth—for the inevitability of change.

She had stayed in industry long after it lost her interest because she was afraid to try something else. To be less than perfect. To disappoint others. To fail.

Now she had the freedom to make her own choices, and that included picking more than one thing if she so desired. She could know her path without knowing exactly where it led. She didn't have to fear the challenges that would come with her choices—she knew she would overcome them. They would change her life or they wouldn't. Either way, she would still be there.

* * *

The Woman had more than just a new project—she had new perspective: as yet another year neared its end, she had finally come to love herself.

The Woman had long been compassionate and loving toward the people in her life. She supported them when they wandered, encouraged them when something sparked their curiosity, and understood when they made mistakes.

But she had not been nearly as compassionate toward herself.

Self-love had never been part of her social conditioning, so she had written it off as silly and frivolous, just as she had initially written off the idea of an all-women's retreat. Once she gave it a chance, however, she saw how transformative a community of women could be. She felt grateful for their support and insights and patience.

It was gratitude that had gotten her to a place of self-love, too. She was grateful for everything in her life: for techniques to lift her spirits and raise her vibe, for family and friends and colleagues and the life-changing souls she hadn't met yet, and even for the moments when she felt like she was back-sliding—lessons she had to learn over and over again, each time with a new layer of understanding.

When she felt grateful for all that she'd been through and all it had taught her, it was impossible not to love herself. The sheer fact of her existence allowed her to have so many rich experiences—the brilliant, painful, thrilling, touching moments that composed her life.

Tapping into the love that she felt shifted her focus, and she began to write. *If not for love, we are lost, adrift in a sea of doing. We lose our souls amid the mindlessness of our many tasks. Now is the time to stop drifting and anchor yourself; now is the time to live in your bliss.*

She had checked many boxes throughout her life. Now, in her notebook, she drew a new set.

❏ Find your vibe
❏ Know your path
❏ Love yourself

She knew that true transformation was never-ending. She would always be looking for her light, attempting to find and follow her inner wisdom. As long as she remained true to herself, it would all work out. This set of boxes would be her big three. These guiding principles—a to-do list to help her keep her eye on her greater purpose—were all she needed to take one step forward on her path.

* * *

It was New Year's Eve. The Woman's husband had long since gone to bed.

She walked into her studio. A year's worth of colorful notes and diagrams greeted her. She took them all down. The Woman was done wandering.

She walked into the sitting room where she and her husband spent hours sharing their life together. She had always loved the room's large windows, which looked out onto the woods surrounding her home. She could tell the seasons from these windows; she could tell the time, too.

As she walked by the windows, the Woman felt called to them. The light of the full moon shone so brightly through them that she couldn't pass up the opportunity to sit and bask in its magnificence.

As she settled herself into her favorite chair, wrapping herself in a warm scarf, her cat at her feet, she closed her eyes and felt a calm come over her. All the years spent tormented by success vanished. All her stress and worry about the challenges ahead disappeared.

*Life is designed to be easy, but recognizing that requires us to let go of all our social conditioning.*

And when she did, all that remained was a woman who had learned to love herself, over and over again, even when she faltered. A woman who had learned that she would become what she believed, and if she trusted the process, she would receive everything she needed.

In that moment of bliss, the moon's light still evident even through her closed lids, the Woman came to realize that there was no right or wrong way to be, as long as she was being herself and listening to the wisdom within. She didn't need to know how to navigate the entire labyrinth of her life; she just had to know she was on the right path and trust herself to take the best next step.

That insight was her true guide. It had been there all along.

With that, the Woman opened her eyes and smiled.

# About the Author

The most important person you will ever meet is you!

PJ discovered this as she walked the labyrinth and realized her incredible strength, unique vibration, and ultimate path along the way. The labyrinth's influence transformed her understanding of herself and the world, and it can do the same for you.

PJ is a one-of-a-kind master of positive vibes. She leverages the labyrinth model to teach women the art of circling to their centers, helping them identify their inner wisdom and their true purpose and learn to love themselves unconditionally throughout the process. As an Awakened Sage, PJ serves as a catalyst for transformation, providing support in one-on-one sessions, group environments, and hands-on labyrinth retreats around the world.

Let PJ show you how to find your unique vibration and awaken the wisdom within. Reach out and connect at www.pjjackson.com.

## Acknowledgments

*G* ratitude is one of the loveliest vibrations we can share with another person, and I am so very grateful to these beautiful souls, who have made a difference in my life and in the writing of this story.

Dearest Rickey, you are the reason I have awakened in so many ways. You were by my side through all that was good and all that was challenging. Your kindness, your support, and your love kept me grounded in myself, and your belief in me gave me the courage to finally let go of the guilt and put myself first.

My baby girl, Elyshia, so much of why this book exists centers on your courage to express yourself, asking me why I put my voice away. Thank you for being my joy, my pride, and my mini-me. Without your consistent encouragement, this book might never have come to fruition.

You may not realize it, Gail Hughes, but you are the spark that lit the fire! Your simple note regarding divine discontent sent me on my spiritual path, and I can never thank you enough. You saw the true me wrapped up inside that business professional even before I did. Thank you for taking the time to share your wisdom with me and help me embrace my awakening.

Chuck Hollingsworth, you are the man who bridged my two worlds, and with such kindness and support. When Rickey got sick and I had to decide it was time to retire, you made that part of this story so fulfilling. You let me know how special I was for choosing my family, even when I didn't know what the future would hold. Your friendship and steadfast faith inspired me to make this transition.

To my biggest fan, Rina Delmonico, you are the original vibe master! Amid all the craziness that life throws at us, you would always stop to meet with me and tell me honestly what worked and what didn't. Your neverending love has been a cornerstone in my life, and for that I will be eternally grateful.

To my three amigos, Tessa Anodide, Emily Maher, and Dawn Hall. Each of you ladies—although you don't know each other—had a special vibration and role in bringing this book to life. Tessa, my dearest mentee, always reading, reviewing, and commenting on every idea I created, thank you for your honesty and your enthusiasm. Emily, my spirit writer, thank you for bringing empathy and love into my writing through our long-distance video calls; you helped me add a voice to my writing that I had hidden. And Dawn, my forever friend, who at a point when I most needed to focus on my fitness, awoke—literally—out of a deep sleep to answer the call, and enabled me to finish my awakening. Thank you, Dawn, for being by my side every week—your connection to spirit enhanced my understanding of this journey called life.

To my partner in prose, Ariel Hubbard, without you this version of my story would never have been born. You are a bundle of love rolled into the most caring, deep listener a writer could ever wish to connect with. You encouraged my ramblings, my crying, and my courage, while helping me craft my words into an exciting and inspiring story. I could not have dreamed how wonderful our relationship would be, and now that we have lived this journey, you are part of my life forever!

And finally, to the unknown woman walking the Labyrinth on April 6, 2018, at the Chartres Cathedral Notre Dame, in Chartres, France. Your voice was heard, and your question, "Am I doing this right?" is why I wrote this book. You may never know just how much your simple outburst in a sea of strangers resonated. You validated why this story is so universally important to so many women—thank you!

CPSIA information can be obtained
at www.ICGtesting.com
Printed in the USA
BVHW042018060619
550071BV00004B/4/P